More Than Anything

Poems by Hiram Larew

VRZHU PRESS · WASHINGTON, DC · 2007

Please direct inquiries to:

VRZHU Press
3323 14th St. NE
Washington, DC 20017
info@vrzhu.com

www.vrzhu.com

Larew, Hiram —
More Than Anything: poems / by Hiram Larew — 1st ed.

Cover and text design by VRZHU Press

FIRST EDITION
ISBN 978-1-4303-1406-6

More Than Anything

THE BRIDGE

Improve me
Make me into a bird bath
Splashing like friends do in the morning
So that I'm ready for most anything

Or have me become
Rotting wood
The kind that's partly wise
And always damp
So that it hardly matters what happens tomorrow

If you can help me at all
Then help me to become the loosest
Doorknob alive
To turn without ever turning
The kind of nuisance
That's like snow is
Whenever it's next to water

Over it all change me into
The fullest why not anyone can imagine
Take me
With no sense at all
To the ripest time to come.

CIGAR

It's as clear to me now
As eggs next to twine
Clear as six is to five -
I know exactly what he thought
Back then
At his age -
Clear as close shaving
Because I have his feet

Moreover of late
Something from then keeps whispering to me
Like snow on a shoulder
It isn't him exactly
It couldn't be
But it's saying up close
To go further

I remember
Deep weeds at the faucet
Hay sacks in the back
And a hillside hardly belonging
But more than anything
There were my string bean arms
That weren't good for much he surely thought
Except his future -
Something about me made him cough

If I do anything now
It's because he said so little
The surest sign of strength
Is quiet
Coming up the steps
And looking at me.

IN HALF

Protect me
Build the safest roof there is
Over me so that when it caves in
I'm looking up
Rock me in some terrific arms of forgiveness
So that I can cause trouble often
Shield me especially in the early morning
From whatever wants to please me
And as I gamble and leak
Run ahead and warn me of what's going to happen
Even when it doesn't
To get completely ready
Plant me upside down
So that as I grow my mind wanders more
Or let me hear fights all around me
Especially the ones that no one ever wins
Take me far away from the fire
When it's cold out
Then wrap me up tight like an orange is
So that I'm never satisfied
Inside.

GO ROUSE JAMES

If every day
In fact if every minute of every day
From now on
Is supposed to be a live-life-fully sort of shock
A kind of emergency of learning
Or a one chance only kind of candy
Then go rouse James
He'd want to be here

For instance
He'd want to look out at those green green branches
Because even as hot and as nervous as they must be
They're still floating on air
And he'd know why and tell us

James was the first person around here
Who got those kind of glasses
(And when he votes he whistles)
And when he smooches ice cubes swirl
Like they're on another planet
James is the kind of person you watch
Because he believes in a movie for as long as it takes
And he'll roam all over outside long before breakfast
Just to listen.

IF HE NEVER HEARS THIS

There's no pattern to what disappears
Nothing to make sure that our ideas are everlasting
Or repeated
In fact we can't predict what stays or lingers
Or leaves
It may be that wishing wells
Especially their walls
Know the secret of this yearning to endure
Somehow fireworks do too coming down
But mostly we know that everything we know
Is just water
And all we are is snaps

Never ask anyone anything directly
Be a swan's neck
So that you find out everything by guessing
And for balance
Imagine loving someone so much that it feels like
You are unscrewing the lid of a jar
And then going

The boring point is this
The best friend to make is chance
Do whatever it takes
To wake up tangled in the arms of maybe
Start to trust what you've done
For as long as a blink
Mostly think like a windy corner.

ALONE

To be like her
To never be enough
To be the kind of striped fish that doesn't stop
To be as smart as a tossed book
To be lifted over corn
To be as shiny as the very top of boyhood
To be a warning
To be a whistling guest
Or spirited soup
To rarely be full or even
To be wrong in a way that's exalted
        for years to come
To gradually become very fragile
To be rice
To be hurried as if only two things mattered
To be really and scared.

HEAP

For the life of me
I can't believe
How so much
Depends on glances or
For that matter
On giving up
But there it is -
Even all of history
And most of what's to come
Is shaped by
Bending grasses and
Some morning's chill
Above us
And all my plans are pauses

If I've been anything
I've been sloppy
With rules like puddles
And with love diced up for the ages
In fact said best
I've been an onion
And still resent deeply
What's proven and known

Enough is enough
By the time you get this
The moon will have changed completely
I'll be a ghost
And farmers
Wonders that they are
Will have started all over again
From scratch.

ALWAYS

Whatever lives in the corner
Whatever someone writes about long afterwards
Whatever seems like half a chance
That's how we ought to be
A try or undiscovered

The greater ideas are the ones
Like a squirrel coming down a tree
That start to think in years
Or see that
We will never be able to make up the difference
Or close the distance
But should try to anyway -
More and more
We sound like bees

Greatness has never depended on staying -
Bump and there is a moon
Lift and there is our time
Through all of the fuss and pushing
Remembering has always been the hardest thing
To leave behind
So is watching now.

AWAY

If on some plover night
Of you
My could have beens alight
Then feather find me
In pretend
With wavy starts and mights

And if you sky
Or if you cry
And as I maybe be
Salt sweet our ever in the once
Fly waking next to me

For I have wished
Hard soft as moons
And always perched in Spring
I know how nothing's sure
Just if
But eyes like yours are wings.

BACK AGAIN

Thanks she wore it in a bun back then
It would fray over cinder paths
Or celery stalks like fringe I see
Mostly I visited as she'd lean down
And I'd poke up with my mouth open
At awe at age and to her smile
She gripped more with simple pans
Or teacher shoes to help me up a stool or pat me
Dusty ways she loved last stooped her door
While I grew out ago.

Then I won't and did forget
Until a million streams
Until one just one so much alike
With chestnut tag of hair
Turned up
But now a he
A hoe
So which is which and bluing eyes
Who is sitting still?

DON'T TELL ANYONE

The hardest thing to do is keep
Or stay
When most of what we do sneaks out
Away
Or turns cousinish on us

Largely put
Ours isn't ours ever
It couldn't be

We need to learn to haven't
To pine for never
To unlove love
To trust the weather.

FARON

Whatever you've hated for so long
Walks up to you one day
While you're busy
Kinda pokes you in the arm
And says it's leaving for good
Next week
If it's really true it's a mixed blessing
Like those very small mirrors
Because it's always good to have some bad around

The ground is so soft just now
That nothing seems fine or fair
Giving way like that reminds you that
To take care of someone else
Is very important
Even if you never will
Even if you're skinny as a rail
Even if dogs go wild as you walk by
Nodding

Holding things in for so long
Can turn you into a kind of anger
That's really like a fight up in a tree
Or a big tooth surrounded by candy
In fact waiting around can be very fitful
More than you'll ever know
Slicking back your hair.

KEEP TRYING TO TELL HIM

Pretend for a minute
That you're a duck
In muddy water
And that whatever's teasing your legs
Is starting to make you nervous

Pretend that you're around sixty
And you're not so sure if you want to know
What's in the message
Even though someone who's skipping
And smiling
Just handed it to you

Pretend that today you'll have the chance
To say whatever's important
Just before something drags the love of your life away
Feet first
Pretend you can tell by the woodsy smell
Out back
That it's now or never.

POURING

I know that
Wintry mountains are much more important
Than this evening
They're meant to be
Our best brothers
But even so
Your eyes
Were more surprising by far -
Like trees on pillows

I believe that anything is possible
And that excitement will always be followed by calm
So really if nothing else gets settled
There's this at least -
I've been you forever

When birds land on edges they scatter some snow -
My hand made the same kind of mistake
It didn't know
That the best part is pouring

Others may disagree
But just once
Is the only because I need
It's over all the if
And wonder
Where does it go as it goes ahead
Why does it always glisten.

SHUDDER

Tell me something so honest it's bald
Make me freeze in place
Stark with snap
Shiny with sudden
Can opened

I can't help the never ending
The water gurgling
The frost growing
The heavens calling
I can only catch some alone
By the ears
And wrestle it down
Until it shudders

There will come a time
When I won't hear from you any more
I'll become a slick floor
And hope will grin up at me like pirates or fairies
The loss of you will be wings
In my face

In an emergency or hoping
The utmost prevails
There's no maybe about it -
I'll never grow up
So throw me a match.

STILL MILK

There are flowers in this part of the world
Called snowdrops
They sprout and bloom so early
When it's still frigid cold outside
That it's a wonder

There are birds here too
Called turkey vultures
That circle large then flop down
To eat dead things
Of any kind

Somehow these two dreams seem connected
Not so much by music
Or even by faith in turns or
Still milk
But by the seams of coal below us
That aren't discovered yet

I believe in what they try to tell us -
That in the mix of spring and all that isn't
The very act of waiting for
Is a lover by itself.

THOU

This shirt will surely end up
Somewhere far away
In a tree maybe
Or beak or even on sand
That will itself turn into mountains one day
Or some tunes out over the crest

But in the meantime
The buttons suppose almost too much of a future
For their own good
And its sleeves act exactly like wind does
In both directions
The back even looks as if it were made
Every stitch
By a window or at least a view

In truth
It's really an ordinary everyday shirt
With an off color nothing more
It doesn't have
Any special loving point about it at all
Except that probably
It won't open
Exactly like this again ever
Will it.

GOLLY

I don't know about you
But when a leafy branch comes in the window
I love it
Beyond common sense
In fact I love anything that's where
It's not supposed to be
And all the air around it

And what I live for more and more
Are the things that shouldn't happen
My best friend is the uh oh sound
Everyone makes
When a glass breaks
And my hero is whispers

One of these days
What I hope to notice first
Before anything else
(Even before eyes)
Is shoulders
Because just like hills
They make me guess
At what I'll never know.

FEATHERS

She may not need me right now
I said to the fence
But one day some day look out
Because she'll be asking for something
Like me
Flaws and all I said
As weeds are rich
Yes
I've surely made mistakes I said
With evening's night and sounds around
But I have always done
Whatever I have done
With the utmost intentions of water
She has made me wholly askance
I said rubbing my head
And it's probably all pointless all this
Like five eggs in a nest I said
Enlarging.

ONE MORE THING

There should be a prize
For the best name in town
For the one that more than any other
Barges in before we're ready
Or acts like prism light does on our face
Or tamps dirt down
Like in a story -
A name that gets things done
Without us

There should also be a big blue ribbon
Right in the middle
For the most enjoyable place we know of
The sort of spot that's muddy with ideas
That won't stay put but for a minute
Somewhere that's deeply lovely
Because it hasn't learned a thing yet
From its mistakes
And smells like ferns do sometimes

Most of all there should be a nice medal
For the kind of friend
Who says so
Even when they shouldn't
Who looks at you up close
And often
As if you're a fool
And thinks of you
Later on long after
By frowning.

SLOW MOTION

Give me time to waste
In buckets dripping with shimmer
So I can see the impossible around me
And live to tell about every kind of pie

Give me the means to be lost
Thrown out into the farthest sky
Like a farmboy or green apples
Waiting to be fully
In fact I'll work at turning my life into
The only nail sticking out of a plank

That will be my job

Your job is everything else -
The stories that roam and swarm around every night
And whatever's too soon to tell
Even more than that
You should make sure there's plenty of worldwide
For me
So that I feel left out in all kinds of ways
Whenever I'm snoring
Please.

WHAT SAY

I'd like to be the guy
Who drives his best buddy
And his wife in a truck
Or better yet a jeep
To the hospital at 2 at night
For her to have their twins
I'd like to strike the match
Cup a couple of cigars
Rub my hair out of my eyes
Smell like smoke
Think of gravy
And how fishing feels
There'd be enough snow
Blowing around on the road
That we'd all shut up
So I could make the turns -
Then some coffee and I'd realize
Having to do with nothing
That I'd half forgotten
My charlie leg.

AUGUST

Who's the best person you've ever met
Out of everyone you've ever known
Who would you pick out

If you say it was the baseball player some summers back
Then you have to say why -
Maybe it was because
Just like seeds and the sky
He felt with all of his might
The power of distance
And kept trying to show it to you

If you say the best person was the widow next door
Then you're also saying how
Every step up leads to autumn
Or even further to a worried wisdom
Because she was your school

Maybe you'll say it was that kid
When you were a kid
Who smelled like straw or a tunnel
Surely of everyone you've ever known
He was most like sandals

Or maybe you'll not think of anyone
Right now as you're loving around
Which is fine
So long as you're good
As a penny.

WELL

You want angry?
I'll give you angry
I'll get you hair burning
Mice squealing toe broken angry
I'll throw it off the roof angry
Smack the moon till it's blue angry
I'll spit words out like a rabid fox
And jab angry in the eyes
Yes indeed I'll make angry angry
You just watch
Twenty years from now they'll still be hollering
Up and down
About my country called angry
And how I discovered it
In my boat called pissed off
Flying its flag with a finger up the middle -
Baby if you want jolly holly
Then keep wiping till you find it
But if you want angry
I'll be right here
Looking like a fist
And sweet as bloody nose pie.

WHAT SCARES ME

I think of you whenever I can see my breath
In the cold
Or have an idea that I didn't expect to
Or whenever I think I recognize someone from behind

I think of you whenever I notice that my hair
Has grown some
Or when I hear birds go over
Or am pouring water out somewhere
Or if I'm inside at night looking out

I try to think of you carefully
I think of you differently
I think of you closely

Any more unless I remember something twice
I won't remember it at all
I think of you whenever a story has come to its middle
Or every time now that my shirt looks better than me.

VERA

If I had four grandchildren and a truck
Like a man is supposed to
And a garden of beans up on the hillside up there
And all the salt that I like
Then I'd probably be even better than I am now

Two or three counties south of here
They leave their doors open
Rain or shine for visits
That's the kind of person I want to be
Ready like an early bird worm -
Spring makes me think longer like that

I've found that most of the time I'm lucky
She says it's my laugh
Well maybe but maybe not
Because last week
Just as I was chuckling
I caught my shoulder on some limbs back there
And thought I was going to pass out
I've never hurt like that before
And hope I never will

Believe me though
That's not really me
I always make the most of what's what
And wait out every up and down
Because I know that by the way and surely
There's always something stewing.

TRAVELING

Do you have any idea
What you mean to me
Because I surely don't
And I never want to
All I want is a smeary sense
Of what you are
Like the only lamp on
In a room

I have no chance at all
Of being equal
Especially when you stutter
Or are not here
Or when you sit down alone to read

Everything I'll most likely do
Started near your nose
And I still just can't believe
How tossed you've made me feel
Like water in a fountain

Promise me this at least
Promise me that for as long as can be
I won't get anywhere close
To what's sure in you.

SLEEPING ON THE FLOOR

I'm only going to say this once
No more than that again ever -
You are one of those rare ones
One of the red rolling over diamonds rare ones
One of the don't need a bed rare ones
The kind that I want who
Doesn't want wanting
So ribbony smart that you're scared
(You should be)
With lips like the number nine
And a grin that's pure lasso
You're wrong as the steepest hill
Cold as whatever twinkles last
And hopeless as an upside down heart
I won't say it any closer than that -
Most likely you and that itch
Wouldn't want me to either.

A PLATE OF COOKIES

Hate is really useful
In a roundabout way -
It's the very rocks in streams
We love
Or the hidden and dried up stem that holds all
The grapes together
And for an eternity and even more
It's the lightning overhead

In the same vein
If no hasn't come by to visit much lately
Then something's wrong
Just ask the little birds on twigs outside
Because they all live with the comfort of worry
And every window around us likes gray

Right down at the core
There's something grown up about ugly
Something that makes sadness completely sure
Taken to its tip what's hurtful is helpful
In fact if there's any doubt about it
Just ask anyone who's nearly finished
Something they've never wanted to do at all.

LOWLY

When I tell you my leg hurts
What I'm saying is that I don't know much
And when I eat poorly at dinner
Just celery
What I'm really doing is wanting some pink vacation
Come on go with me
If I look pale
It's probably because
The beans out front need weeding
If I slip and stutter
It's due to the mean streak in dogs
Nothing has much to do
With what is what
Or how you make me feel except maybe
Fish tails flapping in a bucket
I shouldn't even try to explain
What it's like right now
When there's so little call to.

UP CLOSE

Please be sure of one thing
Be as certain as something floating above
That I'll come back completely
I must I have to —
Over all please stay new and ready
Because this chance this close this hill
So wanting in the distance
So fearful near my hands
Means I will and surely —
There's no other arrow

Never let me leave
And as I'm going
Remember that
Whether far is in the middle
Or I'm all around
There's meant to be
That's under
Stay terribly with me

It's May
Most things are full of wrong and ready
But I'm not sure of what to do
With so much crumbling in the air
I would do anything to see your circle coming round
Please just now be me -
Be me so that somehow I can glimmer back once more
From the other side of rain.

HOPE

For all the cooks
Who in the early morning
Especially the cold mornings
Turn grills on and get batter ready
For them and
For hillsides
Particularly the ones
That slope up just enough
To bring on panting
But not stopping
For them as well and
For wash cloths
The most helpful being cotton and
Old ones
For all of them
Mostly because they are sleepy
In a rousing sort of way.

STUNG

In a few weeks
With freezing frost
This hornets nest
Will be empty abandoned
And then anyone who wants to
Will be able to pull it down if they like
And take it away
To hang it somewhere from a ceiling

Imagine life in that kind of attic
Where quiet turns into old
Where frayed dangling wires are fathers
And the sound of someone scrubbing floors is love -
A place that is full of wings

Surely in all of this world's habits
Through our many comings and goings
And even up over the years
The only spot worth saving can't be won't be
And most importantly shouldn't be -
Bless the home that isn't.

SCARECROW

You don't have enough spit
Even as worlds fly over
And rain comes down
Not enough itch
Not enough salt
Not enough jake
To last

We'll all die like rocks tossed in water
So once and for all
Try to prove what you're worth -
You can't can you
Because every twitch of what's wrong is grinning
And all your rules are just begging to be chased around
Until they pee

There's going to come a time
When tomorrow's not enough -
Leaves will blow back screaming
Cousins will poison
Even fish will take on the shape of hooks
And there you'll be dangling

You won't ever get ready
But after all why should you
When the sun hasn't changed since puck
And the moon is just mud

Listen to this like you look -
When you can't figure out what smells
Take some advice
And leave.

READY OR NOT

Why are uncles special
All charmed to themselves?
And why my surprise?

I suspect if I had had one early on
I would have watched him like smoke
Every strange visit of his
And worn my pants differently, some ribbons.
From him I would have realized roles sooner
As he skated ahead.
Because at the start an uncle is a twirl of breath posing
Gay as a faun at a fountain
No cares at all
And later is as clever as clues
A compass
Or proof that can't can be.
Uncles - when no one else dares.

All of this is important because I realize
Ready or not
That I am an uncle
That some lost kid hopes on my wings.
And I realize that when he asks me for paints or a wand
That's nice
But what he'll really need are schemes and hooves.

LAST

You are not with me
For lettuce or life -
But if there's an ever
Or gifts pure as logs over water
With the wonderful smoke of belonging
Then please promise in all and in every
In simple in finally
That I will remember you
Near me.

CUFF

The last thing I was was bad
And the next thing I'll be is worse
I'm foregone and predestined
Like rusted scissors
So it doesn't matter if start stops
Or girls boy
I'm natively wrong
And my punishment is
To have a string run from
My mouth up to the very sky
So that I have no secrets at all
And so that I really do know better

My idea of perfect is confusion -
Flies finding a carcass
Lips trying to yell under water
Or gravity crazy mad at its equal
I like messes
And whatever throws a fit
I like mud even up on the ceiling

As I've said
Just give me one good reason
Why I shouldn't enjoy fumes or snakes
Or anything that's out of control
Tell me why disaster shouldn't be a friend
You see here's what it really comes down to -
My dead is better than yours
And I'll bet the whole stash on it
Even as all of the big brown cows
Go floating down by us
In the river.

ROUGH

There's a spot in your heart
You won't get to ever
No matter how green the gold
And so sometimes
If you can't fall asleep
You should go out to your island
Where you won't likely forget
That you do make a difference
Like a bean does

More in the sense of overlapping waves
Be by the way
In what you can do
So that no matter
What tends to happen
There's a lovely roughness
With you some.

BLOEMFONTEIN

The most important word there is anywhere
Is imagine
It's the cause of all skies and milk
Never ending
As well as the ups and downs it takes
To build yes
Forever overlooking
It's even the echoey who cares
Upon which nose bleeds depend.

Beyond reason you also understand that
The most crucial sounds in the world
Aren't words at all
And never have been
And that's why they are
Your very best friends.

No matter what else happens
You must give up your place
So that you're completely after
Even ransom your heart
Trade in your days
Turn over every hope you've imagined
To end up next
And just be
Naked like grass overflowing
Or certain as wood in a blaze.

A POET'S FUNERAL

The boy who was there
Will always be the boy who
        was there
He was not there at all but was there
        to remember
And was gone as if he had never been there
        or about
But was here near the near of tomorrow
Coming nearer to here or
        then there -

He was the boy of tomorrow and never
        was there
Or could be about but in all of tomorrow
        he was the boy
Who was there and will always be near
        as if
Tomorrow was here
So he was tomorrow not always
But then again
He was the boy who
        will always be here
Nearer and nearer to there.

LANKY

I'm warning you
Don't listen to me
Because if you do
You'll end up crisp
Without any hope of earning some
          perfumy or big stuff merit
You'll become all afar
And skinny as a feather

Having said that
I'd suggest that you dig out under the fence at night
Leave good advice behind – lonely crazy
And head out with a headache
Take every dumb turn that you can
Go for all of the deadends
Then buzz buzz buzz like you are dying
So that that way
What I just said
Right here right now
Won't make any difference
At all
Ha!

PINK ROSES

Here are the facts as I know them –
The feet you hate are the feet you get
So be it amen

And so be the case
That every silly stitch you really need
Doesn't need you –
Not the shiny pennies down in grass
Surely not that heave ho over to there
And not even someone smeary
In fact too much of you is others

It's also hard to yell and cook
          At the same time
But it's done the world over
By lightning by witches by love

That's enough of this for now
Except to say that
The end smells
Just like the beginning -
Here
Take a sniff.

ALDO

I love you in the wrong way
The way spit feels in water
Or how dogs dream
I love you like hornets
And here's why –
You're the skid marks of ancient history
The whoop of every bad morning
Even the smash and cries of my very best crimes
I just don't like what I like
And you're the worst like of all

Yea well so…

Let's make a deal
I'll give you sixty three reasons to misunderstand me
And then you can give me no glue at all
Not a drop
That way we can call it even
Together
Eye to eye
Ashes to ashes
And never everlasting.

LIFE WITH A CANDLE

I want to marry this field
Truly and simply
With its wings curving the corners
And its smoothness stunning my knees
My heart is here far around me
And it's humming and leaning —
Even the trifling breeze

I want this field for my living
To vow to its edges
That nothing comes true
Without greening
Nothing seems as bold as my longings
Except sloping
Nothing wakes on my shoulder
But rustling
I hope the strangest hopes in this field
Ever bending

From here
I know that this much of my all is clear -
Before there were hills
Or even eyes to up over
There was a distance beyond us
A long far away that can never come near
There was wishing

I want to carry this field
In my arms
By its being and dust
To a maybe that's certain
So our future flickers on grasses
And our children will wave from the clouds.

IN PASSING

Over the ever fields
Hovering just above the green and rainings
My ancestors from every country alive
Squint bird-like to see me
Or tie loops to finish their calling
And then rows upon rows of bending
They pull me up onto their backs
Over the ever fields
And take me into the skins of apples
The spreading of limbs
The grains of my longing —
This is to say I say to myself
Where I will be coming.

In passing
I see how all of the otherwise matters —
There's the sweet wasted edge of the fields at last
And the life I've always been after
That's half way between the law and the wind
In the end
If I am an orphan or wrong
It's the tree-type kind
That doesn't know any better
Someday I say out loud to myself
I will be careful
But not just yet
Not with the fields cloudy with spirits and daring.

World that there is
There's little to keep me
No onions or signals or low leaning skies
And as much as I'd like to
I'll never be branches out over
The fields of my families and betters.

No this part of the ages is pulling and tugging me
As soup does to history
As land does to eyes.

About the Author

Hiram Larew's work has appeared in several journals and books including *the washington review, Rhino, Rue Bella, The Cosmos Club Journal, Frantic Egg, Not Just Air,* and *Echoes*. Nominated for a 2006 Pushcart Prize, his poems have been recognized for awards by, among others, *Louisiana Literature, Verve,* the Allen Ginsberg Awards, and *S. S. Calliope*. As an advocate for the diversity of poetic voices, he has read widely across the U.S., and assembled this collection while at the Virginia Center for the Creative Arts.

As the co-founder of the The Poet Connection, Larew lives in Upper Marlboro, Maryland, and directs international farming programs for the U.S. government.

About VRZHU Press

VRZHU Press is committed to presenting the very best writing available to them in modern poetry. We are committed to creating beautiful pieces of visual/verbal art that you can enjoy and treasure.

We are very proud to present *More Than Anything* as the first of what we hope will be many volumes of vibrant modern poetry. For more titles from VRZHU and to find out more about us, visit us at our website at www.VRZHU.com

Or write us at: VRZHU Press
3323 14th St. NE
Washington, DC 20017
info@vrzhu.com

This book was laid out in Adobe Jenson Pro and Myriad Pro with titles in Nicholas.

www.ingramcontent.com/pod-product-compliance
Ingram Content Group UK Ltd.
Pitfield, Milton Keynes, MK11 3LW, UK
UKHW041836200726
13854UKWH00003BA/1169

9 781430 314066